When Herdsmen are Kings

First Edition

Copyright © Uzoma Nduka, Ph.D

All rights reserved.
Published by The Lighthouse books, Agape Inc.

No part of this book may be reproduced, stored in a retrieval system, or transmitted in any form or by any means, electronic, mechanical photocopying, recording, or otherwise without written permission of the publisher.

For information regarding permission, write
thelighthousemain@gmail.com
ISBN: 978-1-950320-11-0

Visit us at:
www.thelighthousebooks.com
Printed in the USA

When Herdsmen are Kings

THERE USED TO BE A TIME
WHEN HERDSMEN WERE
NOT HEARD OF,

THEY USED TO LIVE IN
FORESTS WITH COWS AND
STICKS AND CHARMS

BUT NOW HERDSMEN ARE WITH HUMANS ON ROADS, AND STREETS, AND FARMLANDS.

DESTROYING ALL THAT'S PLANTED.

THE MAIZE, THE YAMS

THEY STROLL THE STREETS
OF CITIES,

AND BLOCK THE ROADS TO
CARS.

THEY TAKE OVER THE
SCHOOLS.

AND LIVE THERE WITH
THEIR COWS.

THERE'S SOMETHING CALLED A RANCH.

THAT'S WHERE CATTLE'S ARE KEPT.

THEY GRAZE THE GRASS RIGHT THERE.

AND TRULY FEEL AT HOME.

THE LAND OF PEACE AND LOVE.

WHERE ALL WILL LIVE AS ONE.

THE LAND OF MANY TRIBES.

THERE LIES HER STRENGTH AND POWER.

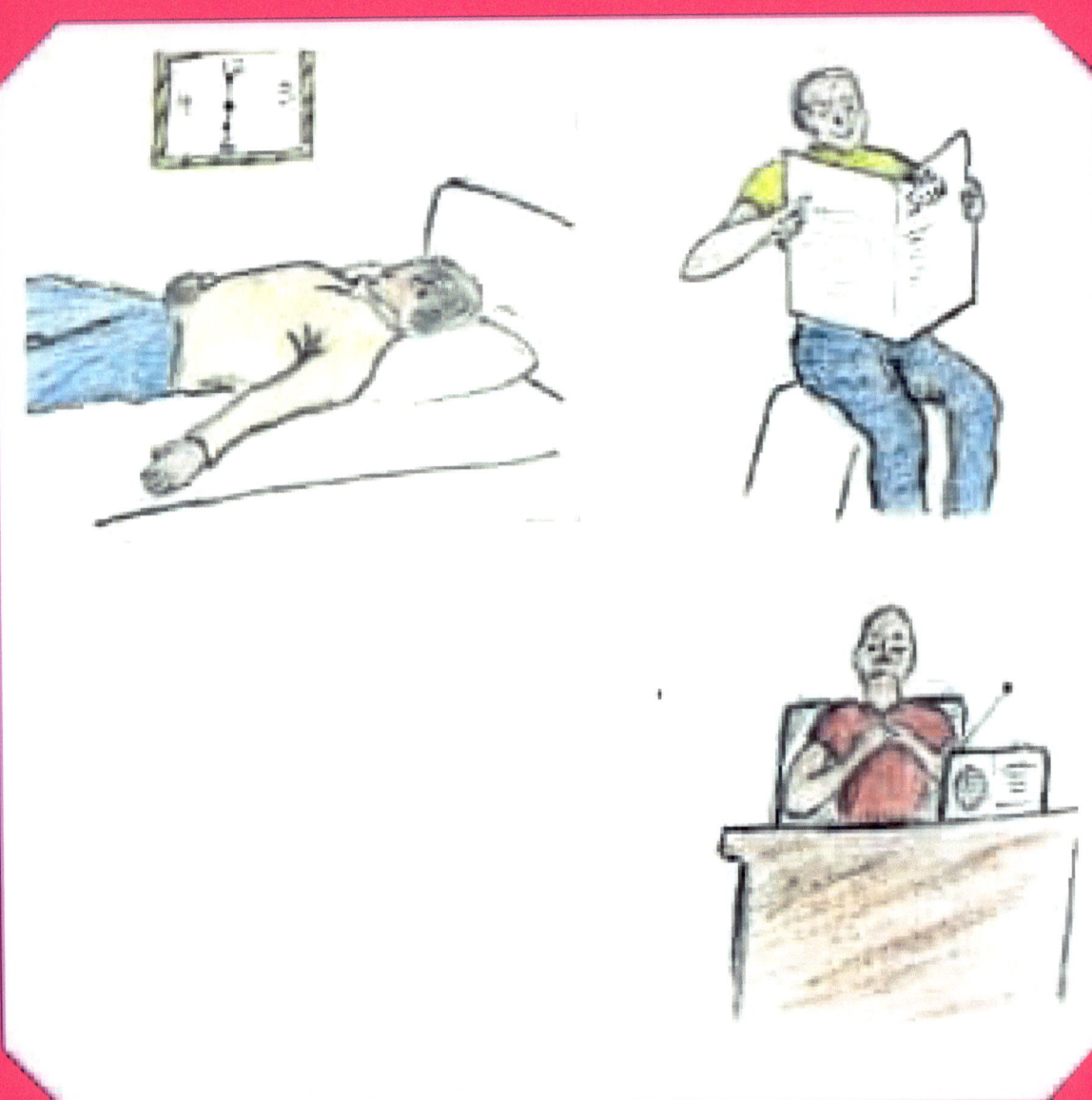

A TIME WE SPOKE OUR MINDS.

A TIME WE SLEPT IN PEACE.

A TIME WE WALKED WITH NO FEAR.

A TIME WE HAD NIGERIA.

A COUNTRY CALLED NIGERIA.

WHERE TRIBES AND TONGUE MAY DIFFER YET. STOOD AS ONE SOME TIMES.

BUT NOW THINGS AREN'T THE SAME.

A TIME WHEN LIGHT WAS STEADY.

A TIME WHEN PHONES DID WORK.

A TIME OUR FLIGHTS DID FLY.

A TIME WE WERE AS ONE.

YET, NO ONE SEEMS TO LISTEN.

THEY CARE ABOUT ELECTIONS FOR THEM TO STEAL SOME MORE.

THIS TIME WE'LL ELECT OURSELVES

HERDSMEN AND FARMERS FIGHT.

AND NO ONE SEEMS TO CARE.

IT'S TIME WE KIDS RISE UP

AND SAY HERDSMEN AREN'T KINGS!

TEN PEOPLE KILLED LAST NIGHT.

A HUNDRED KILLED TODAY.

THOUSANDS MAY DIE TOMORROW.

AND WHEN WILL ALL THESE END?

WE'LL MARCH ON THE STREETS OF ABUJA.

WE'LL CLOSE OUR SCHOOLS AND SCREAM WE'LL FORCE THE MOSQUES TO CLOSE.

AND CHURCHES TOO WILL CLOSE.

It seems no one is listening.

That's what I see from Dad's face.

It seems all hope is lost.

His mood does show me that.

IT'S TIME FOR US TO WAKE UP.

IT'S TIME FOR US TO SPEAK UP.

WAKE UP AND TAKE OUR COUNTRY.

SPEAK UP AGAINST THIS EVIL.

IT'S TIME WE KIDS RISE UP.

AND SAY HERDSMEN AREN'T KINGS!

About the Author

Uzoma C. Nduka Ph.D is a seasoned writer and poet.

He was educated at Abia State University, Uturu, University of Nigeria, Nsukka and Metropolitan State University of Denver.

He also went to George Washington University, Harvard Medical School, and Walden University where he obtained a Ph.D. in Epidemiology.

His earlier works include Trees of Discomfort, School Bell, The Cuban Boy.

Dr. Uzoma currently resides with his family in Denver, CO, USA.

www.ingramcontent.com/pod-product-compliance
Lightning Source LLC
Chambersburg PA
CBHW040028050426
42453CB00002B/46